The HMS *Wager*: The History of the 18th Century's Most Famous Shipwreck and Mutiny

By Charles River Editors

An 18th century depiction of the wreck

About Charles River Editors

Charles River Editors is a boutique digital publishing company, specializing in bringing history back to life with educational and engaging books on a wide range of topics. Keep up to date with our new and free offerings with this 5 second sign up on our weekly mailing list, and visit Our Kindle Author Page to see other recently published Kindle titles.

We make these books for you and always want to know our readers' opinions, so we encourage you to leave reviews and look forward to publishing new and exciting titles each week.

Introduction

Cape Horn

The HMS *Wager*

"Whereas upon a General Consultation, it has been agreed to go from this Place through the Streights of Magellan, for the coast of Brazil, in our way for England: We do, notwithstanding, find the People separating into Parties, which must consequently end in the Destruction of the whole Body; and as also there have been great robberies committed on the Stores and every Thing is now at a Stand; therefore, to prevent all future Frauds and Animosoties, we are unanimously agreed to proceed as above-mentioned." – John Bulkley, gunner on the HMS *Wager*

"I cannot suppose the Captain will refuse the signing of it; but he is so self-willed, the best step we can take, is to put him under arrest for the killing of Mr. Cozens. In this case I will, with your approbation, assume command. Then our affairs will be concluded to the satisfaction of the whole company, without being any longer liable to the obstruction they now meet from the Captain's perverseness and chicanery." – Lieutenant Robert Baynes, second-in-command on the HMS *Wager*

Mention the 18th century Royal Navy and visions come to mind of swashbuckling sailors swinging from rope to rope while a red-faced captain in an even redder coat and a powdered wig shouts order and pitches fits. Such visions, largely shaped by Hollywood pictures such as the popular *Pirates of the Caribbean* franchise, naturally fail to do full justice to a group of men who functioned, with little direction and even less support, on the seas for years at a time. Disney may enjoy portraying them sitting down to sumptuous feasts or cavorting with scantily clad native girls, but the opposite was true; the men were almost always hungry, with even the best meals consisting of little more than bread, beans, and a bit of meat on the side if the voyage was still in its early days. Likewise, those stranded on islands were not met by pretty native girls bearing coconut cream pies but instead cold and wind and an unremitting surf that drove away both flora and fauna.

Those who doubt this reality or unfamiliar with it need only consult the journals and records of the officers and crew of the HMS *Wager*, who sailed from England to fight the Spanish in 1741 and instead ended up fighting for their lives. These men, many of whom were already long past the normal age of service, endured short rations and rough seas for months, only to end up shipwrecked on an island off of South America. Many died during the wreck, as did many others who were marooned, only to discover it bare of almost all supplies necessary for survival. On top of those tribulations, mutinous men rose up violently against their captain and made their way across more than 2,000 miles of tossing seas in an open boat. Their trip was characterized not just by hardship and hunger but also by that most dastardly of crimes – betrayal - as their leaders again and again chose their own good over that of their men.

Of the almost 100 men that set out on the *Wager*, only a handful made it home, and even then they returned not together but piecemeal after having been separated by their troubles. When they finally did make their way back to England, they came home not to a hero's welcome but numerous questions and ultimately a court martial. For a number of reasons, ranging from lack of evidence to prosecutorial reluctance, the men were not convicted of any crimes; in fact, most of the survivors went on to have successful careers in the British Navy and other endeavors. However, no rational person could ever claim that they got away unpunished, for surely the sights of friends dying slowly of starvation and dead bodies piled on beaches for carrion to attack were tougher punishments than the Admiralty could ever mete out on them.

The HMS Wager: The History of the 18th Century's Most Famous Shipwreck and Mutiny chronicles one of the most notorious chapters in the Royal Navy's history. Along with pictures of important people and places, you will learn about the shipwreck and mutiny like never before.

The HMS *Wager*: The History of the 18th Century's Most Famous Shipwreck and Mutiny
About Charles River Editors
Introduction
   Chapter 1: A Harrowing Voyage
   Chapter 2: A Harrowing Shipwreck
   Chapter 3: A Harrowing Mutiny
   Chapter 4: The Mutineers' Journey Home
   Chapter 5: The Return of Captain Cheap's Group
   Chapter 6: Court Martials and the Aftermath
   Online Resources
   Bibliography
Free Books by Charles River Editors
Discounted Books by Charles River Editors

Chapter 1: A Harrowing Voyage

In the 21st century, it can be difficult to comprehend the risks taken by early sailors who set out to sea in ships so small they could comfortably sit on the deck of a modern aircraft carrier or luxury liner. These men sailed for months and sometimes years without being able to contact their families, and often they went nearly as long without setting foot on land. Expeditions in the first few centuries of the Age of Exploration could often find themselves entirely dependent on their wits to survive, as there was little chance of getting outside help if something went wrong.

The ship later known as the *Wager* began her life as an East Indiaman, also known as a "tea clipper," because its main purpose was to carry tea harvested by the East India Company from India to England. Though that sounds like an innocuous duty, it was actually dangerous work, as evidenced by the fact she was armed with nearly 30 guns. She and her crew of around 100 men made several trips back and forth to India between 1735 and 1739, when the British Royal Navy bought her from her owner, a J. Raymond, for use by Commodore George Anson in patrolling the west coast of South America.

Anson

The ship's new owner sent her right on to the Navy shipyard, where through the winter and spring of 1739-40, the Royal Navy spent more than £7,000 fitting her out for naval service. She resumed work on April 22, 1740 as the *Wager*, named not because of any card game but in honor of Admiral Sir Charles Wager, who was sponsoring the voyage. Though well-equipped with guns, the *Wager* was designated a sixth-rate and would be used primarily to carry small weapons and gunpowder, as well as 120 men and 28 guns.

Wager

By this time, Britain was once again at war with Spain, and with that in mind the Duke of Newcastle sent Commodore Anson, with the *Wager* and five other ships, to South America. Newcastle was known to be more of a puppet than a leader, to the extent that historian Harry Dickinson once described him as "notorious for his fussiness and fretfulness, his petty jealousies, his reluctance to accept responsibility for his actions, and his inability to pursue any political objective to his own satisfaction or to the nations profit ... Many modern historians have depicted him as the epitome of unredeemed mediocrity and as a veritable buffoon in office." Therefore, it is quite likely that he was acting at the behest of someone else, perhaps Hubert Tassell or Henry Hutchison, two agents of the South Sea Company who stood to make quite a bit of money if Britain could run the Spanish out of South America. Not only did they sell the Navy supplies for the ships, they also devised a way to join the sailors on their fateful journey, a decision they would undoubtedly come to regret.

Newcastle

Newcastle's ordered Anson "to use your best endeavours to annoy and distress the Spaniards, either at sea or land, to the utmost of your power, by taking, sinking, burning, or otherwise destroying all their ships and vessels that you shall meet with, and particularly their boats, and all embarkations whatsoever, that they may not be able to send any intelligence by sea along the coast of your being in those parts." Furthermore, he told the captain, "In case you shall find it practical to seize, surprise or take any of the towns or places belonging to the Spaniards on the coast, that you may judge worthy of making such an enterprise upon, you are to attempt it; for which purpose we have not only ordered the land forces above mentioned, but have also thought proper to direct that an additional number of small arms be put on board the ships under your command…"

The people that Anson was ordered not to attack were the indigenous peoples, but this was not based on any sense of morality. Newcastle explained that "the number of native Indians on the coast of Chile greatly exceeds that of the Spaniards, and that there is reason to believe that the said Indians may not be averse to join with you against the Spaniards in order to recover their freedom, you are to endeavour to cultivate a good understanding with such Indians as shall be willing to join and assist you in any attempt that you may think proper…"

Writing in 1885, historian John Knox Laughton observed that Anson's mission seems to have been doomed from the start: "The establishment of the navy…and the expense of fitting out the fleet for the West Indies and the coast of Spain swallowed up all the resources of the admiralty. There was thus great difficulty in equipping and manning the ships intended for the Pacific; whilst instead of the regiment of soldiers…a number of pensioners, old, worn-out, and crippled, were put on board, together with a number of newly enlisted and wholly undrilled marines…All this caused great delay, and it was not till 18 September 1740, after eight months' preparation, that the little squadron of six ships put to sea from St. Helens."

It is hard to imagine the physical condition of most of these men, as 18th century people did not retire young to play golf. Those living on their pensions were doing so because they were no longer considered able to work any normal jobs to which they may have been accustomed. Now these men, many of whom were in their 60s and 70s, were being loaded up and sent to endure life aboard leaking, creaking vessels that regularly killed younger, stronger men.

Nevertheless, the king needed warm bodies and no one was exempt; indeed, those too frail to climb the ladder up the side of the ship were hauled up in slings. Anson himself later wrote of these unfortunate men that "the most crazy and infirm only should be culled out for so laborious and perilous an undertaking…whereas the whole detachment that was sent…seemed to be made up of the most decrepit and miserable objects that could be collected out of the whole body; and…these were a second time cleared of that little health and strength which were to be found amongst them…" Perhaps not surprisingly, they proved to be more of a liability than an asset, because it only took a few months before some of them began to die during the voyage, requiring the others to take time out to bury them at sea. Given the various fates that would befall the crew, it is little surprise there are no records of any pensioners aboard the *Wager* making it back home to England.

Regardless, all of these men, along with the younger and healthier sailors, were packed onto the six warships and two transports that set out in August 1740. Weighing in at over 1,000 tons and crewed by 400 men, the *Centurion* was the largest. Then there were the twins, *Gloucester* and *Severn*, both the same size and carrying the same number of men and guns. The *Pearl* was only slightly larger than the *Wager* but carried twice as many men and 40 guns. There was also the little *Tryal*, with a crew of 70 and only eight guns. Sailing along beside the fearsome warships were the *Anna* and *Industry*, carrying additional food and tools for the voyage.

A contemporary painting of the *Centurion* (background) fighting a Spanish ship

When the ships set out on their expedition, none of the British crewmembers were aware that the delays had allowed the French to find out about the expedition and tell the Spanish government. In turn, the Spanish sent its own small flotilla to intercept the men at Madeira. Fortunately for the Spaniards, if not Anson and his men, they had plenty of time to get there, because various troubles plagued the trip enough to delay the British ships' arrival until October 25. However, the British sailors were lucky enough to manage to slip in and out of the port without the Spanish catching them.

As it turned out, that was the first and probably last time fortune smiled on the voyage. Just weeks later, after the *Industry* left to return to England, the warm air began to take its toll on their supplies, and the food started to rot. Moreover, the ships were overcrowded, and while this was a situation that the men normally coped with by spending as much time as possible on deck, the rotting food brought flies, which spread germs throughout the ship and led to an outbreak of typhus. The sick men were subsequently confined to crowded quarters, where the disease spread, bringing with it the scourge of all armies: dysentery.

The crew continued to grow more ill by the day, but finally the ships sighted land just a few days before Christmas and were able to anchor off Santa Catarina Island, along the coast of Brazil. Anson ordered all the sick men ashore, where they were able to recover in fresh air and sunshine, with fresh water and fresh fruit to eat. While they were off the ship, he ordered those remaining behind to scrub down the lower decks and build smoking fires in each compartment to drive out the vermin. He then had men use vinegar to wash down the walls and floors on every level.

Had the ships been able to follow Anson's original plans to get into port, clean up and get out again, all would have gone well. Instead, he ordered all seven ships to remain there for a month while the *Tryal* was repaired. This meant that the men were exposed night and day to malarial mosquito bites, which killed as many men on shore as might have died in the holds of the ship. In fact, when the ships finally left Santa Catarina Island on January 18, 1741, they carried away more sick men than they had brought to shore.

Anson's troubles did not end here, for just a few days later the ships ran into bad weather so severe that it broke the *Tryal*'s newly repaired mast off and crippled the ship. Anson ordered the *Gloucester* to tie off her crippled sister and tow her behind the rest of the party, slowing down everyone's progress. The group also lost the *Pearl*, which drifted off course and away from the flotilla during the storm. Her captain died during the process and was replaced by First Lieutenant Sampson Salt, who was so desperate to find his compatriots that he mistakenly signaled a Spanish flotilla led by José Alfonso Pizarro (not to be confused with conquistador Francisco Pizarro). The *Pearl* managed to escape and reunite with the English ships, but only by throwing everything possible overboard in order to lighten the load.

Pizarro

After stopping briefly for repairs at St. Julian, the British ships sailed on toward Cape Horn, encouraged by improving weather. In March 1741, Anson ordered the *Tryal* to take the lead, charging her crew with spotting any ice that was ahead. Already damaged and poorly repaired, the *Tryal* was no match for the job and had to be replaced by the *Pearl*, leading Captain Saumarez of the *Tryal* to drearily record in his journal that "really life is not worth pursuing at the expense of such hardships."

As if starvation, thirst, dysentery, typhus and storms were not enough, the men also began to feel the effects of scurvy, a dreaded disease that afflicted sailors for centuries. Caused by a lack of Vitamin C, it decimated Anson's men during the weeks they spent trying to round Cape Horn. To make matters worse, the severe storms left even the best navigators in the crew unable to calculate exactly where the ships were in relation to the land.

Thus, it came as a shock when, on the night of April 13, a sailor standing watch on the *Anna* looked across the sea and saw the high cliffs of Cape Noir outlined by the moonlight only a couple of miles away. The *Anna* fired warning shots and waved lanterns just in time to warn the other ships off, and a chaplain aboard the *Centurion* would write of Cape Noir, "It was indeed most wonderful, that the currents should have driven us to the eastward with such strength; for the whole squadron esteemed themselves upwards of ten degrees more westerly than this land, so that in running down, by our account, about nineteen degrees of longitude, we had not really advanced half that distance. And now, instead of having our labours and anxieties relieved by approaching a warmer climate and more tranquil seas, we were to steer again to the southward, and were again to combat those western blasts, which had so often terrified us; and this too, when we were greatly enfeebled by our men falling sick, and dying apace, and when our spirits, dejected by a long continuance at sea, and by our late disappointment, were much less capable of supporting us in the various difficulties, which we could not but expect in this new undertaking."

As fate would have it, the escape from this close call would prove to be only a short respite from danger.

Chapter 2: A Harrowing Shipwreck

On the night of April 23, just 10 days after avoiding near disaster, an even stronger storm hit, and this one managed to scatter the ships and rip the *Wager*'s sails to shreds. In anticipation of such an event possibly occurring, the various ships had been given rendezvous points to meet back up if they got separated, and of the three potential rendezvous points, Anson would end up sailing to the Juan Fernández Islands off the coast of Chile. In addition to the *Wager* being blown off course, the *Severn* and *Pearl* also got separated, and the captains of those ships eventually decided to return across the Atlantic back to England without trying to link back up with Anson.

Meanwhile, the *Wager*'s captain, David Cheap (who had been promoted after Captain Dandy Kidd had died aboard the ship before reaching Cape Horn), had difficulty not only navigating the ship but simply sailing it, thanks to the damage done by the storms and the poor condition of the men on board. With so many disabled by illness, the *Wager* barely had more than a dozen fit men able to operate the ship, and Cheap made the mistake of trying to head for a different rendezvous point than Anson. Ironically, Cheap, despite being mostly confined by his own sickness, overruled suggestions that the *Wager* head for the Juan Fernández Islands.

As it turned out, the *Wager* would not sail far enough west to reach the rendezvous point before the ship was steered north, getting itself lost in a bay the sailors knew nothing about. Captain Cheap later wrote miserably of how the ship was wrecked in the early hours of the morning of May 14 on the rocks around Patagonia. The weather, he said, was foul (in fact, they were in the midst of a hurricane), and the ship had already lost her mizzen-mast, making it nearly impossible to sail in the fierce winds. Most of the soldiers were sick with scurvy or dysentery or both, and everyone was hungry and very thirsty. He was himself in very poor shape, recalling that "on the afternoon before the ship was lost, as I was walking along the deck…to give some directions about repairing of four of the chain-plates...I was thrown down one of the hatchways, and was so unlucky as to dislocate the upper bone of my left arm. I was taken up very much stunned and hurt with the violence of the fall and dislocation, which cost the Surgeon two or three hours of trouble to reduce, and bring me to myself."

Ever mindful of the needs of his men, Cheap sent for his second-in-command, Robert Baynes, and his gunner and warned them about the dire situation. He also gave them orders that he later claimed would have saved the ship, only to be ignored: "But my Lieutenant [Baynes]...went...to his bottle, without giving himself any farther concern about the preservation of His Majesty's ship. The Surgeon, contrary to my knowledge, laid me asleep with an opiate.... So that I knew nothing of what was doing in the ship...till half an hour past four next morning, the time when the ship first struck, although my Lieutenant had orders...to inform me if we had any ground with the lead, and of the winds and weather."

Awakening to find the ship stuck on the rocks, the captain, no doubt still compromised by the opiate he had been given, could do little but remain with his sick crew as the waves pounded the ship. Cheap wrote that he was "expecting the ship every moment to go to pieces." The rudder broke and knocked a hole in the bottom of the ship, flooding the lower levels but not knocking her from the rocks.

When the sun rose, he saw that they were stranded off the coast of the Cordillaras islands. With no other alternative presenting itself, the men decided to try to make their way ashore. Midshipman Alexander Campbell later recalled Cheap's noble reply when he offered to help his injured captain ashore: "His answer was, Go and save all the sick, and don't mind me. He also gave orders for hoisting the boats out as soon as possible.... I observed that this very day, the spirit of discord and dissension had entered the people. When I required some of them to return with me in the yawl, to fetch such things from the ship as were necessary for every man...they plainly answered, that they would not go." Campbell did go back for his captain, assuring him that everyone else who wanted to had already headed for shore. What Campbell did not mention was that, because they were so sick and weak, some of the men never made it but were instead swept away by the waves.

On the other hand, Campbell did report that food was scarce and shelter almost nonexistent. Campbell would write, "There was on the island two or three huts built by the Indians.... One of these was fixed on for the Captain; and happy for him it was, that any habitation could be had: for in his condition he had certainly lost his life without such a shelter, as many of the people afterwards did. As soon as the Captain got into this hut, he ordered me to take the yawl, and see if the men on board would come ashore."

Unfortunately, it seems that Cheap's concern for his crew was, perhaps, too little too late, for when Campbell arrived back at the ship, he "found them all in such confusion as cannot be imagined." The men had helped themselves to the ship's weapons and liquor, and they were completely intoxicated. Campbell explained, "Some were singing psalms, others fighting, others swearing, and some lay drunk on the deck. ...[O]bserving some casks of ball and powder on the quarterdeck, I began to put them into the boat; whereupon two of the men came to me, crying out, 'Damn ye! You shall not have them, for the ship is lost and it is ours.' A third came with a bayonet, swearing he would kill me; ...he threw the bayonet at me...I immediately...returned to the shore."

A number of these men perished on the ship itself, their minds likely broken by the effects of scurvy and unlimited alcohol. Among the handful of sailors who survived on the vessel was one John King, who soon put himself forth as their leader. As historian Alan Gurney observed, "The first thing that strikes one when reading the narratives is the complete and utter breakdown of authority aboard the Wager. Suddenly, at a stroke, the strict hierarchical discipline of the Royal Navy tumbles into total anarchy. The scenes aboard the grounded vessel, her masts cut down and her hull pounded by waves, are ones straight out of the Grand Guignol. Men break into the weapon chests and arm themselves with swords, muskets and pistols...Brandy and wine barrels are broached and drunks reel around the deck, some to fall down hatches and then drown in the flooded bilge. Some men sing Psalms, other fight. One man is murdered, strangled to death. This bacchanalia becomes Surrealist when men break open the merchandise chests containing clothing, and then parade the deck wearing velvet coats, laces and ribbons over their soiled canvas trousers and shirts."

Chapter 3: A Harrowing Mutiny

Perhaps it was just as well that the men had a few last laughs, because most of the 140 men who did reach land would not live for long as the weather and other conditions drained the last life out of their already fragile bodies. One of the men who did survive the ordeal, a Mr. Jones, later recalled, "Whichever way we looked a scene of horror presented itself. On one side the wreck (in which was all we had in the world to support and subsist us), together with a boisterous sea, presented us with the most dreary prospect; on the other, the land did not wear a much more favourable appearance: desolate and barren, without sign of culture, we could hope to receive little other benefit from it than the preservation it afforded us from the sea. It must be confessed this was a great and merciful deliverance from immediate destruction; but then we had wet, cold, and hunger to struggle with, and no visible remedy against any of these evils. Exerting ourselves, however, though faint, benumbed, and almost helpless, to find some wretched covert against the extreme inclemency of the weather, we discovered an Indian hut at a small distance from the beach within a wood, in which as many as possible without distinction crowded themselves..." Fittingly, the men had found themselves stranded on what was soon to be known as Wager Island.

Even this shelter would prove to be but poor comfort, as Jones also noted that "here our situation was such as to exclude all rest and refreshment by sleep from most of us; for besides that we pressed upon one another extremely, we were not without our alarms and apprehensions of being attacked by the Indians, from a discovery we made of some of their lances and other arms in our hut; and our uncertainty of their strength and disposition gave alarm to our imagination, and kept us in continual anxiety."

Those who were strong enough to do so built simple shelters out of cloth that the ship had carried to trade with the native peoples, and while the living found precious little to eat, there was plenty of rum rescued from the ship's stores to drink. Soon, they were spending more and more time numbed to their surroundings by the comfort and false warmth the alcohol provided, and before long, many joined their other fallen comrades.

Perhaps inevitably, the breakdown in cohesion and the anger many survivors harbored toward Cheap for the wreck set the stage for a mutiny. Order broke down entirely, and men began to fight to the death over the most meager rations. King added to the tension by insisting that those who had reached shore should risk their lives to return to the ship and pick him and those who were still alive up. When Cheap failed to move fast enough to suit him, he fired on the captain's hut, putting a four pound cannonball through the top of it.

Tragically, the men might have been rescued right away had the weather not been so bad as to prevent them for seeing the *Anna*, which traveled near them along this time. As Anson later put it, "I cannot but observe how much it is to be lamented that the *Wager*'s people had no knowledge of her being so near them on the coast; for as she was not above thirty leagues distant from them, and came into their neighbourhood about the same time the *Wager* was lost, and was a fine roomy ship, she could easily have taken them all on board, and have carried them to Juan Fernandes." He added sorrowfully, "Indeed, I suspect she was still nearer to them than what is here estimated; for several of the *Wager*'s people, at different times, heard the report of a cannon, which I conceive could be no other than the evening gun fired from the Anna pink, especially as what was heard at Wager's Island was about the same time of the day."

Meanwhile, Cheap, still recovering from his wounds, believed that they must travel north if they had any hope of rejoining the other English ships. Most of the men disagreed, wanting to instead travel south in hopes of finding a more hospitable island on which to recover. The men who disagreed were led by gunner John Bulkley. He suggested that if the ship's carpenter, John Cummins, could enlarge the longboat, it might be converted to a schooner. Along with the cutter and the barge, this might allow the men to sail for the Strait of Magellan and from there, home. Cheap considered his proposal for a time but ultimately turned it down, insisting that the men had a duty to try to find Anson and complete their mission. If he failed to do so, or at least to try, he could himself be charged with dereliction of duty, or even worse, cowardice, a capital offense.

Although his own warrant officers spoke out on behalf of Bulkley's plan, Cheap remained resolute, exhibiting a determination that ultimately led to mutiny. Of course, mutiny was also a capital offense unless the mutineers could later justify their decisions before a military court, so the men began to put together a case for their actions even as they planned them.

Their first justification for what they were doing was based on a fear of personal safety claim after an incident involving Captain Cheap shooting an intoxicated crewmember in early June. Had Cheap allowed the man to sober up and then flogged him, no one would have thought much of it, but no captain, even in the most dire straits, could reasonably be expected to pull out his pistol and shoot a man in the face. Midshipman John Byron, whose personal memoirs still remain one of the most popular accounts of the *Wager*'s travails, described the incident in defense of the part he played in the mutiny: "Mr. Cozens was at the store-tent; and having, it seems, lately had a quarrel with the Purser, and now some words arising between them, the latter told him he was come to mutiny; and without any further ceremony fired a pistol at his head, which narrowly missed him. The Captain, hearing the report of the pistol, and perhaps the Purser's words that Cozens was come to mutiny, ran out of his hut with a cocked pistol, and without asking any questions immediately shot him through the head."

Naturally, everyone, including Byron, came running to see what the gunfire meant. Byron continued, "[What] I saw was Mr. Cozens on the ground weltering in his blood. He was sensible, and took me by the hand, as he did several others, shaking his head as if he meant to take leave of us." Appalled by what he witnessed that day, Byron wrote, "If Mr. Cozens' behaviour to the Captain was indecent and provoking, the Captain's on the other hand was rash and hasty. If the first was wanting in that respect and observance which is due from a petty officer to his commander, the latter was still more ill advised in the method he took for the enforcement of his authority, of which indeed he was jealous to the last degree, and which he saw daily declining and ready to be trampled upon."

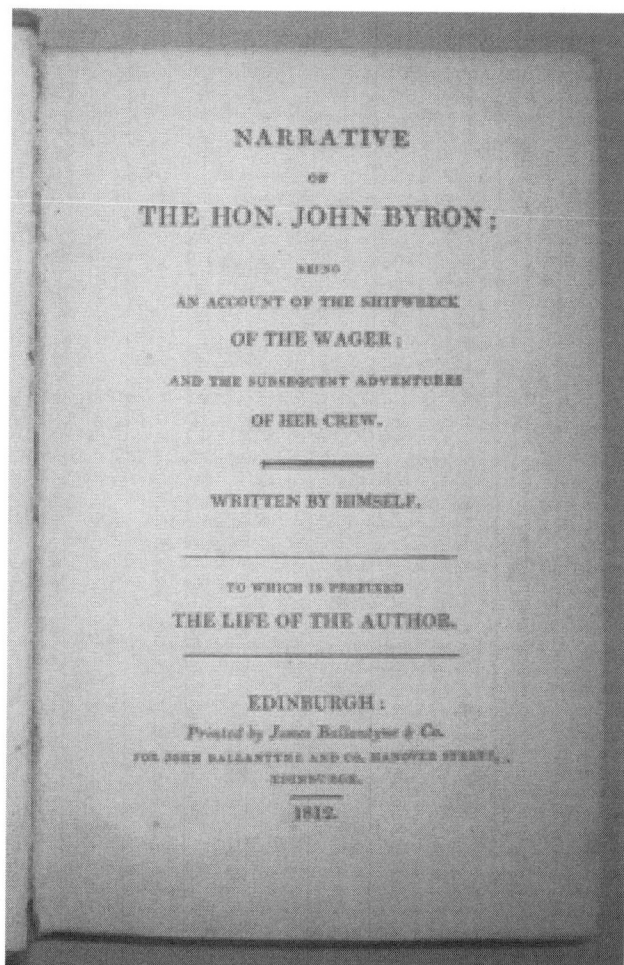

The cover page of an edition of Byron's memoirs

To make matters worse, the man in question, Cozens, did not die right away but instead lingered for 10 days. Cooper, whose account was at least somewhat sympathetic to the captain, nonetheless recorded, "After the extraction of the ball the wound dressed kindly, and there was a likelihood of his recovering. Hereupon he expressed an inclination of being moved to the tent where he had lodged before this mischief befell him. The Gunner and Carpenter, whose tent that was, not presuming to act in this matter without the Captain's permission, waited on him for that purpose, earnestly praying him to indulge the sick man's desire."

Here was a chance for Cheap to show some remorse for his hasty action, but Cooper could only report, "But so far was he from condescending to what they most reasonably asked, that he vehemently replied, 'No. The scoundrel shan't be gratified.' ... The people propagated the disaffection from one to another in their cabals, muttering it would be more honourable of him to dispatch the prisoner at once than force him thus to languish out his miserable hours in a doleful cold wet place, dying as it were by piecemeal."

In reference to Cheap's apparent cruelty, Cooper could only say that "the Captain's austerity, in respect of Cozens, might not proceed from inhumanity or mere resentment…but from an apprehension of its being fitting at that time and in those circumstances to behave with intrepid steadiness, and to betray no symptom of irresolution or weakness. On Wednesday the 24th instant this unfortunate contentious fellow expired, after lingering fourteen days from the time of his being wounded. His shipmates buried him with all the decent formality their situation would then admit of."

Pointing to the Cozens incident as the turning point that ensured the subsequent mutiny, Byron concluded, "[Cheap's] mistaken apprehension of a mutinous design in Mr. Cozens, the sole motive of his rash action, was so far from answering the end he proposed by it, that the men, who before were much dissatisfied and uneasy, were by this unfortunate step thrown almost into open sedition and revolt. It was evident that the people…were extremely affected with this catastrophe of Mr. Cozens…. Their minds were now exasperated, and…their resentment…would shortly show itself in some desperate enterprise."

By the time Cozens was dead and the schooner was completed, a confrontation was inevitable. It came when Bulkley presented Cheap with a document that read as a clear ultimatum: "Whereas upon a General Consultation, it has been agreed to go from this Place through the Streights of Magellan, for the coast of Brazil, in our way for England: We do, notwithstanding, find the People separating into Parties, which must consequently end in the Destruction of the whole Body; and as also there have been great robberies committed on the Stores and every Thing is now at a Stand; therefore, to prevent all future Frauds and Animosoties, we are unanimously agreed to proceed as above-mentioned."

When he read the letter, Lieutenant Baynes, who had previously been loyal to Cheap, surprised the men by saying, "I cannot suppose the Captain will refuse the signing of it; but he is so self-willed, the best step we can take, is to put him under arrest for the killing of Mr. Cozens. In this case I will, with your approbation, assume command. Then our affairs will be concluded to the satisfaction of the whole company, without being any longer liable to the obstruction they now meet from the Captain's perverseness and chicanery."

The mutineers took Bayne's words as a suggestion. According to Bulkley, "Friday the 9th, this morning went in a body and surprised the Captain in bed, disarmed him, and took everything out of his tent. ...The Captain said, gentlemen, do you know what you have done, or are about? He was answered, yes, sir; our assistance was demanded by Captain Pemberton, to secure you as a prisoner for the death of Mr. Cozens; and as we are subjects of Great Britain, we are obliged to take you as such to England."

If Bulkley's account was accurate, it appears Cheap was more than willing to give his men the benefit of the doubt and believe that they were more mistaken than truly mutinous. Either way, Bulkley continued, "The Captain said, gentlemen, Captain Pemberton has nothing to do with me; I am your commander still; I will show you my instructions; which he did to the people. On this we came out. ... I could not think you would serve me so. It was told him, sir, it is your own fault; you have given yourself no manner of concern for the public good…but have acted quite the reverse…as if we had no commander…"

Had they stopped there, the men might never have been charged with mutiny, but they took further steps, including locking up Marine Lieutenant Hamilton. Though taken aback, Cheap maintained his wits enough to quip, "Well 'Captain' Baynes! You will doubtless be called to account for this hereafter."

Chapter 4: The Mutineers' Journey Home

In the wake of the mutiny, 81 men left the island on October 13, 1741, 5 months after being shipwrecked, in the schooner they called *Speedwell*. Bulkley tried to get Cheap to go with them, but the captain refused, and the leader of the mutineers was more than happy to leave him behind to suffer what he felt sure was an imminent death. However, The *Dublin Gazette* later quoted Bulkley as claiming, "Provision deliver'd to the captain, surgeon, and lieutenant Hamilton, with eight deserters, which last are to be at half allowance of the quantity made out to the people: which make the whole number seven at whole allowance. To the captain, surgeon, and lieutenant Hamilton, six pieces of beef, six pieces of pork, and ninety pound of flour: For the deserters, eight pieces of beef, eight pieces of pork, one hundred weight of flour."

One must indeed marvel at Bulkley's description of those who chose to remain with their captain as "deserters." But an even bigger lie was yet to be told, for the *Gazette* next quoted him as saying, "As soon as the above things were deliver'd we got ready for sailing. I went and took my leave of the captain; he repeated his injunction, That at safe return to England, I would impartially relate all proceedings; he spoke to me in the most tender and affectionate manner, and…desired me to accept of a suit of his best wearing apparel: At parting, he gave me his hand with a great deal of cheerfulness, wishing me well and safe to England."

No man would dare to tell such an obviously false story unless he felt quite certain that no one who knew the truth would live long enough to tell it. In fact, Bulkley made it clear that he believed Cheap to be dead, even as he insisted that he hoped the former captain was alive: "This was the last time I ever saw the unfortunate captain Cheap. However, we hope to see him again in England, that Mr. Cummins and myself maybe freed from some heavy imputations to our prejudice laid on us by the gentleman who succeeded him in command, and who, having an opportunity of arriving-before us in England, not only in the place he touched at abroad, but at home, has blackened us with the greatest calumnies..."

Among them was Midshipman Isaac Morris, who documented the early days of the *Speedwell*'s treacherous voyage: "[W]e put to sea in our longboat and cutter...leaving Capt. Cheap and nineteen others on Wager Island.... Our design was to steer alongshore, through the Straits of Magellan, to the coast of Brazil, which, though a desperate undertaking in such a part of the world, remarkable for tempestuous winds and tumbling seas, we engaged in it with the utmost cheerfulness, being buoyed up with the hopes of once more seeing our native country."

The mutineers seemed to be cursed from the very beginning. Shortly after setting sail, the barge that they took along with them kept splitting its sails, resulting in Bulkley ordering a number of men, including Byron and Campbell, to take it back to Wager Island and hang it with new rigging. According to Cheap, he greeted the men warmly and easily persuaded them to stay behind with him and await rescue, though Campbell, more than a little inclined to paint himself as a hero, told a slightly different tale: "On the 17th, being now out at sea, I had an opportunity of speaking to the people that were with me in the barge, and represented to them, what a shame it was to leave their captain in such a situation; and added, 'That if they did get home, which they could not reasonably hope to do the way they were going, they would be hanged for mutiny; but if, on the other hand, we should go back to the captain, and with him to the northward, we had a much better chance.'"

Campbell continued on by explaining how he just so happened upon the luck needed to make his plan work: "My discourse wrought upon most of them, and they consented to go back; but at the same time objected to our want of provisions, and observed, that it would be dangerous to ask those in the boat for any, lest they should take the barge from us. However...it luckily happened that Mr. Bulkley...ordered me to return with the barge to Wager Island...and to bring off a tent belonging to Captain Pemberton, of the marines, which he said he should want, to make sails for the boat."

Campbell even took credit for taking Byron along, adding, "I observed to the. Hon. Mr. Byron...that now was the time, if he had a mind to go back to the captain. This he immediately resolved to do, but was afraid our new chiefs would suspect our intention, and stop our voyage: but they did not, and we happily got safe to Wager Island that night, where the captain gladly received us."

However it happened, Byron, Campbell, William Harvey, David Buckley, William Ross, Richard Noble, Peter Plastow, Joseph Clinch, Rowland Crusset, and John Bosman all headed back to Wager Island and stayed put. It did not take long for Bulkley to wonder what had become of his men, and since he did not think they had been lost at sea, he decided to return to Wager Island in an effort to find them. By the time Bulkley and the other mutineers arrived, Wager Island had been deserted.

Now down to only two small ships, Bulkley returned to his southward course, but he seemingly failed to take into consideration that a crew made up of mutineers could hardly be counted on to remain loyal to their new captain. Thus, he was caught by surprise on November 3 when the crew of the cutter abandoned the schooner to make their own way. Without the cutter, there was no way for the men to make land and forage for food.

Despairing of survival in the frigid south, the men of the *Speedwell* rallied to some small hope when, just a few days later, the cutter rejoined them, but only days after that, the cutter broke loose in the night and floated quickly to shore, where she wrecked on the rocks. Bulkley, who had judged Cheap so harshly, had lost 1/8th of his crew during his first two weeks in command, but he still couldn't feed everyone he still had left, so he marooned 10 other poor men along the southern coast of Chile.

Now with only 60 men left to provide for, Bulkley finally made it to the notorious Strait of Magellan, where he quickly realized that a small crew, while easy to feed, was hard-pressed to successfully navigate the treacherous waters, as everyone remaining had to stand lengthy watches and learn jobs that they had not been trained for in the past. Morris later recalled, "In our passage several of our companions were starved to death, and those of us who survived were so miserably reduced, through want of nourishment, that we had scarce strength to do our duty. … On January the 10th, 1741-42, almost destitute of provisions, we were blessed with the agreeable prospect, distant about seven leagues. …we saw a great many wild horses and some dogs."

These otherwise unappetizing sources of protein looked pretty good to the starving men, and 14 of them thought strong enough to make it to shore set out swimming for the island on January 12, 1742. 13 of them would make it, with one of them proving unable to make it. Morris closed his account of this incident with the following words: "After we had walked about a mile in from the beach, we saw a great number of wild horses and dogs…. There were large flocks of parrots about the rocks, and near the waterside a few seal. We likewise met with a good spring of fresh water…. We shot a wild horse and some seal, and filled three casks with fresh water…. Soon after which the schooner stood farther off at sea, the sea breeze blowing strong."

A few days later, Bulkley sent another 8 men ashore along the coast of Patagonia, ostensibly to gather water, and then left them behind on the island, reducing his crew to 33. After another week or two, 30 starving men finally made it to shore on the southern coast of the Brazil. They had travelled 2,500 miles in the improvised craft and were soon able to arrange passage aboard the *Saint Catherine*, a brigantine that, while far from luxurious, must have seemed so to men who had spent 15 weeks sailing in some of the roughest seas in the world in an open craft. They were welcomed warmly by Portugal's royal governor, a meeting Bulkley recounted in his account: "The Governor...told us we were more welcome to him in the miserable condition we arrived than if we had brought all the wealth in the world with us. ...he fully assured us that he would dispatch us the first opportunity to Rio Janeiro; and whenever we stood in need of anything, he ordered us to acquaint the Commandant, and our wants should be instantly supplied. He then took leave of us, and wished us well."

In spite of this warm welcome, the mutineers' troubles were far from over. In short order, the 30 castaways found that they had traded deadly waters for equally dangerous political and bureaucratic red tape. While Bulkley tried to negotiate passage for his men back to England, John King, always the troublemaker, devoted himself to leading a group of disenchanted shipmates in harassing Bulkley and the others, leading them to finally relocate in order to get away from him. According to Captain S.W.C. Pack, "As soon as the ruffians had gone, the terrified occupants left their house via the back wall and fled into the country. Early the next morning they called on the consul and asked for protection. He readily understood that they were all in mortal peril from the mad designs of the boatswain [King] and placed them under protection and undertook to get them on board a ship where they could work their passage."

Finally, on May 20, Bulkley and his followers set sail on the *Saint Tubes* for Bahia and then Lisbon. On October 1, the British Consul there reported, "Last week four officers of the Wager which went out with Mr. Anson...two lieutenants of marines and four sailors arrived here in a Portuguese vessel; they say they were cast away upon an uninhabited island in the South Seas in May last...after they had lost their ship they lengthened their longboat and threw a deck over her in which & two open boats the whole crew being 81 in number resorted to put to sea, except their Captain..." The consul innocently passed on Bulkley's lie that Cheap refused to sail with them because he thought the ship would be unable to make the trip.

The consul also sent back other information about the mutineers' harrowing return to Europe: "One of the boats put back..., the others proceeded, sailed the Straights of Magellan, kept along the coast 'till they got to Rio Grande, where they say they were well received by the Portuguese. But before they got there several of the people died in the voyage.... The rest sailed again from thence and went to Rio de Janeiro, what numbers landed there they do not remember. ...Lieutenant [Baynes] says...the sailors were become masters and would not suffer him to keep a journal." The fact Bulkley had intentionally marooned a number of sailors was conveniently omitted.

The consul concluded his report by writing, "When they got to the Rio de Janeiro...lots of their companions who left them at Rio Grande had been there & were gone away in His Majesty's ship commanded by Captain Smith who sailed for the West Indies seven or eight days before they got in. The officers gone home of this Packet [i.e. HMS Stirling Castle] & the sailors are put on board His Majesty's ship the Greyhound."

Once in Spain, the men were able to book passage to England, where they arrived on the first day of 1743. By the time they arrived, Baynes had already started to regret his involvement in the affair and immediately went to the Admiralty so that he might tell his side of the story first. The problem was, of course, that as the senior officer among the mutineers, he automatically bore responsibility for the actions of the men under his command.

Fortunately for Baynes, the Admiralty was not inclined to blacken the name of such a high ranking officer and instead ordered that Bulkley and Cummins be arrested and held on HMS *Stirling Castle* until they could decide whether or not to charge them with any crime. It did not help their cause that they had recently co-authored a book which claimed to be "a faithful Narrative of the Loss of his Majesty's Ship the Wager, on a desolate Island.... With the Proceedings and Conduct of the Officers and Crew and the hardships they endur'd in the said Island for the Space of five Months; their bold Attempt for Liberty, in Coasting the Southern Part of the vast Region of Patagonia; letting out with upwards of eighty Souls in their Boats; the Desertion of the Crew with the Barge; their Passage through the Streights of Magellan..." The book also contained "an Account of their manner of living in the Voyage on Seals, wild Horses, Dogs, &c. and the incredible Hardships they frequently underwent for Want of Food of any Kind; a Description of the several Places where they touch'd in the Streights of Magellan, with an Account of the inhabitants &c. and their safe Arrival to the Brazil, after sailing One Thousand Leagues, in a Long-Boat...." But wait, as the saying goes, there's more, including details related to "their Reception from the Portuguese; an Account of the Disturbances at Rio Grand; their Arrival at Rio Janeiro; their Passage and Usage on Board a Portuguese Ship to Lisbon; and their Voyage to England. Interspers'd with many entertaining and curious Observations, not taken Notice of by Sir John Narborough, or any other Journalist."

Not surprisingly, all of Britain was fascinated by the story. The *Dublin Gazette* published an excerpt describing the natives encountered by the returning crewmen: "The Indians we saw in the Straits of Magellan are people of a middle stature and well-shaped, their complexion of a tawny olive colour, their hair exceeding black, but not very long, they have round faces and small noses, their eyes little and black, their teeth are smooth and even, and close set, of an incomparable whiteness...they are very alive in body, and run with a surprising agility, they wear on their heads white feather a caps, their bodies are cover'd with the skins of seal and guanacos. The women, as soon as they saw us, fled into the woods, so that we can give no description of them." Bulkley and the others would soon enough have a chance to give a more detailed description of the people of the New World, as some of them would prove critical to their chances of being freed.

After considering what to do with Bulkley and Cummins for two weeks, the court decided to release the men pending the arrival back in England of either Anson or Cheap, either of whom, it was assumed, could give a corroborating or conflicting account of events.

Anson made it back to England in 1744, but he was obviously unable to shed any significant light on the events that took place after he lost sight of the *Wager*, so the court decided to wait for Cheap. For Bulkley, this must have seemed to be the end of all his troubles, as he never expected to see his former captain alive again. In fact, he felt so sure of his position that he sold his journal to a local publisher and awaited the accolades he felt would surely follow its release. Even as many believed there was no way to describe his actions as anything other than mutiny, the lack of formal charges against him allowed him to quickly be put in command of the *Saphire*, a privateer ship. The London papers soon began reporting his escapades with relish.

Chapter 5: The Return of Captain Cheap's Group

Much to everyone's surprise, Cheap did make it back home, reaching his native shore on April 9, 1745, and if possible, his group's return was just as perilous and adventurous as Bulkley's group.

After months stranded on Wager Island, Cheap and the others decided to take the two ships they had left, the barge and the yawl, up the South American coast and try to make their way to Chile. They soon lost the yawl to bad weather and faced the dreaded situation of not having enough room for everyone to continue the voyage. Campbell remembered, " "The loss of the yawl was a great misfortune to us who belonged to her (being seven in number) all our clothes, arms, etc. being lost with her. As the barge was not capable of carrying both us and her own company, being in all seventeen men, it was determined to leave four of the Marines on this desolate place. This was a melancholy thing, but necessity compelled us to it. And as we were obliged to leave some behind us, the marines were fixed on, as not being of any service on board. What made the case of these poor men the more deplorable, was the place being destitute of seal, shellfish, or anything they could possibly live upon. The captain left them arms, ammunition, a frying pan, and several other necessaries."

This left 14 men crowded onto the small barge, but the crew still couldn't make any headway and eventually opted to return to Wager Island two months later. Perhaps discouraged by his men's disloyalty or just too tired to keep on trying, Cheap lost all his sense of duty at this point and began to spend his time laying about and fighting with the others over his ration of food.

The men remaining at this point might never have made it home had a group of natives not come to their rescue about two weeks after they had returned to Wager Island. The natives guided the British sailors to a Spanish settlement, but the overland journey took its toll on the already weak men and only four ultimately made it to safety: Marine Lieutenant Hamilton, Campbell, Byron, and Cheap.

The English sailors reached Chaco, but their troubles were still far from over. At that Spanish colonial possession, they were held prisoner by the town's governor for seven months, though their ordeal there was not nearly as bad as it might have been since they were housed with local families and pretty much given the run of the area. In fact, so comfortable were their surroundings that Byron soon found himself with a new problem: he caught the eye of an older woman who was not inclined to let him leave her home. He later wrote, "Whilst we were at Castro, the old lady…sent to the governor, and begged I might be allowed to come to her for a few weeks; this was granted, and accordingly I went and passed about three weeks with her very happily, as she seemed to be as fond of me as if I had been her own son. She was very unwilling to part with me again, but as the governor…sent for me, and I left my benefactress with regret."

It turned out this was far from the end of Byron's lady problems, for he again caught the eye of a young woman, this one said to be the wealthiest heiress on the island. She apparently begged her uncle to set up a match, and Byron reported, "As the old man doted upon her, be readily agreed to it; and accordingly, on the next visit I made him, acquainted me with the young lady's proposal, and his approbation of it, taking me at the same time into a room where there were several chests and boxes, which be unlocked, first shewing me what a number of fine clothes his niece had, and then his own wardrobe, which he said should be mine at his death." While the young sailor held strong against these temptations, one nearly took him in: "Amongst other things, he produced a piece of linen, which he said should immediately be made up into shirts for me. I own this last article was a great temptation to me; however, I had the resolution to withstand it, and made the best excuses I could for not accepting of the honour they intended me, for by this time I could speak Spanish well enough to make myself understood."

Byron may have come to regret spurning the powerful uncle's offer, because on January 2, 1743, he and his comrades were transferred to Valparaiso, where the officers were placed in custody at St. Jago and he and Campbell were thrown into a horrific jail. Not only did they have to endure rats and lice, they were also harassed nearly daily by visitors who paid good money to come and look at them, so terrible were the reputations of Englishmen. After a time, some of these same people became so sympathetic to their plight that they actually began to bring them food and small amounts of cash, with which they were eventually able to buy their way into more comfortable surroundings in Santiago.

It seems that Byron's charms once more came to their aid, as Campbell later noted: "The Spaniards are very proud, and dress extremely gay; particularly the women, who spend a great deal of money upon their persons and houses. They are a good sort of people, and very courteous to strangers. Their women are also fond of gentlemen from other countries, and of other nations."

After two years living among the Spanish, the four men finally had the chance to head home, but Campbell refused to travel with the others because he had fallen out with Cheap over money. Thus, while Cheap, Hamilton, and Byron set sail on March 1, 1745 on the *Lys*, a French ship,

Campbell chose "to embark in a Spanish man-of-war then lying at Buenos Aires."

Cheap and his party made it as far as Brest, in France, before once again being abandoned. From there, it took them six months to find passage back to England but they finally made it home on April 9, 1745.

This left only the poor souls at Freshwater Bay still unaccounted for, but they too would live to tell their tales. They lived in Patagonia for a month, surviving by killing and eating the seals along the coast. Rested and strengthened by a steady diet of protein, they began an arduous 300 mile journey to Buenos Aires, fearful the entire trip of the Tehuelche Indians who lived in the area. At one point, they managed to walk 60 miles in two days, only to have to turn around and return to the bay because they could find no water inland.

The marooned survivors remained there until May 1742, by which time the seals had become fearful of humans and were no longer so easy to kill. At this point, they decided that they were likely going to live out the rest of their lives there, so they managed to trap some wild pigs that they bred and domesticated. This plan seem to be working until the predatory cats on the island got scent of penned up meat and began stalking the men's village.

While these four legged enemies made the men nervous, they were actually in more danger from the two-legged variety. Weeks later, a hunting party returned to camp to find that the men left behind had been murdered and the camp itself ransacked. This was enough to compel the four men who survived to quickly pack up what little they had left and start out again for Buenos Aires, this time with two pigs and 16 dogs they had managed to tame and raise.

Once again, they were forced to return to the bay, and again they tried to make lives for themselves there, but this time, the men who had previously attacked their camp returned and captured the four Englishmen to hold as slaves. Considered something of a novelty, they were owned by a number of men before finally becoming part of the household of the chief of the tribe. The chief managed to communicate with them enough to learn that they were English and sworn enemies of Spain. Since he was also at war with the Spaniards, he felt a kinship with them and provided better care for them. By the time 1743 came to a close, they had convinced him to help them return to England. He agreed, though he insisted that he would keep one of them, a mulatto named John Duck, in his household. At around this time, another Englishman, a trader, heard about the three who wanted to go home and paid the chief $90 each to release them.

This apparent salvation was short lived. When the men arrived in Buenos Aires, they were arrested again, this time by the Spanish governor, who demanded that they become Catholic. A few months later, in early 1745, a Spanish warship made it into port and took the men prisoners, chaining them up with a diet of bread and water for more than three months before releasing them.

In a strange twist of fate, Campbell himself arrived in Buenos Aires at about this time, having finally completed his harrowing, five month long trek across the Andes. He, too, was jailed by the Spanish, but he decided to convert to Catholicism, if only to enjoy better food and wine. He then used his influence to arrange passage home for himself, Morris, Cooper and Andrews.

The four men left for Spain in late October 1745, on board the *Asia*, where the three had previously been held prisoner. Incredibly, the men got a taste of déjà vu when 11 Indian crewmen mutinied and killed or injured 40 Spanish crewmen, but with a crew of more than 500, the captain was able to take back control, killing the chief mutineer and inspiring the others to jump overboard and, presumably, drown.

When the *Asia* finally arrived in Corcubion in January 1746, the Spanish authorities once more threw Morris, Andrews and Cooper in jail, and they hauled Campbell inland to Madrid. This led to rumors flying that Campbell had actually defected to the Spanish Navy, but he ultimately returned to England in May 1746, less than two months before his three other comrades finally made it home. Nonetheless, Campbell was still drummed out of the thoroughly Protestant British Navy because of his newfound religion. He blamed Cheap for much of his hard luck and later wrote, "Most of the hardships I suffered in following the fortunes of Captain Cheap were the consequence of my voluntary attachment to that gentleman. In reward for this the Captain has approved himself the greatest Enemy I have in the world. His ungenerous Usage of me forced me to quit his Company, and embark for Europe in a Spanish ship rather than a French one."

Chapter 6: Court Martials and the Aftermath

Naturally, when he got back, Captain Cheap wasted no time in going to the Admiralty and demanding that Bulkley be court martialed. The Admiralty readily agreed and ordered all those involved with the case to report to the HMS *Prince George*, anchored at Spithead, for the proceedings.

Ever the sneak, Bulkley invited the Deputy Marshal of the Admiralty to dinner but neglected to give him his real name. Bulkley later recalled what he said to him at dinner: "Desiring to know his opinion in regard to the Officers of the Wager, as their Captain was come home; for that I had a near relation which was an Officer that came in the long-boat from Brazil, and it would give me concern if he would suffer: His answer was that he believ'd that we should be hang'd [sic]. To which I replied, for God's Sake for what, for not being drown'd? And is a Murderer at last come home to their Accuser? I have carefully perused the Journal, and can't conceive that they have been guilty of Piracy, Mutiny, nor any Thing else to deserve it. It looks to me as if their Adversaries have taken up arms against the Power of the Almighty, for delivering them." According to Bulkley, the Deputy Marshal replied, "Sir, they have been guilty of such things to Captain Cheap whilst a Prisoner, that I believe the Gunner and Carpenter will be hang'd if no Body else." Thinking he had found an ally, Bulkley then admitted his true identity, only to learn that he had overplayed his hand, for the Deputy Marshal arrested him on the spot and transported him to the *Prince George*.

Vice Admiral James Stuart opened the proceedings on Tuesday, April 15, 1746. A number of witnesses came forward and told the story of what happened during the events leading up to Patagonia, but Cheap decided, under the advice of counsel, not to go after Bulkley and the others, for fear that this would raise the issue of Cozens' murder. The men in turn insisted that since they could no longer be paid after the *Wager* was wrecked, they were no longer obligated to obey orders. Captain S.W.C. Pack later wrote his own record of the trial and observed, "Their Lordships knew that a conviction of mutiny would be unpopular with the country. Things were bad with the Navy in April 1746. Their Lordships were out of favour. ... The defence that the Mutineers had was that as their wages automatically stopped when the ship was lost, they were no longer under naval law. Existence of such a misconception could lead, in time of enemy action or other hazard, to anticipation that the ship was already lost."

A decision supporting this theory could result in serious repercussions during a time of war, when men captured might claim that they no longer owed their country allegiance. In fact, Anson, who became a Lord Commissioner the following year, pushed through an Act that declared 'for extending the discipline of the Navy to crews of his majesty's ships, wrecked lost or taken, and continuing to receive wages upon certain conditions...''

In the end, it wasn't the law that saved the mutineers but simply the fact that the British public, which had been so taken with the survival stories, clearly did not favor strict punishment. Pack concluded, "Their Lordships knew that a conviction of mutiny would be unpopular with the country. Things were bad with the Navy in April 1746. Their Lordships were out of favour. One of the reasons for this was their harsh treatment of Admiral Vernon, a popular figure with the public... The defence that the Mutineers had was that as their wages automatically stopped when the ship was lost, they were no longer under naval law. Existence of such a misconception could lead, in time of enemy action or other hazard, to anticipation that the ship was already lost. Anson realised the danger and corrected this misconception. As Lord Commissioner he removed any further doubt in 1747. An Act was passed 'for extending the discipline of the Navy to crews of his majesty's ships, wrecked lost or taken, and continuing to receive wages upon certain conditions... The survivors of the Wager were extremely lucky not to be convicted of mutiny and owe their acquittal not only to the unpopularity of the Board, but to the strength of public opinion, to the fact that their miraculous escapes had captured the public fancy."

Thus, one by one the mutineers were acquitted until only Baynes remained accused, not of mutiny but of failure to carry out his duty and save the ship from floundering in the first place. However, the Admiralty was inclined to sweep even that matter under the rug. Their decision ultimately declared that "the Court, having maturely considered the case of Lieutenant Baynes, are unanimously of opinion that he was to blame in not acquainting the Captain when the Carpenter told him he thought he saw the land, in never heaving the lead, nor letting go the anchor..."

Moreover, the judges were men who in their time had faced all sorts of dangers, and they noted there were mitigating circumstances, including "the weakly condition of the ship, the cable being foul, and but thirteen sickly hands to clear it, as well as the little reason he appeared to have to believe it could have been the land which the Carpenter fancied he saw, either from its appearance, or from the distance his own & the general reckonings of the ship made them from the land..." As a result, "the Court do adjudge him the said Robert Baynes to be acquitted for the loss of the said ship Wager, but to be reprimanded by the President for such omission, & he is hereby acquitted accordingly, & ordered to be reprimanded."

For his part, Cheap was considered a hero, his treatment of Cozens considered secondary to his devotion to duty and his loyalty to the crown. The Admiralty promoted him to Post Captain, a rank that put him on the fast track for Admiral. He captured a large enemy ship in 1748, and the booty awarded to him from that ship made him a wealthy man. He had little time to enjoy his riches, however, as he died in 1752.

The other men were equally unlucky. Baynes' career at sea ended with the *Wager*, and he died in 1758. Bulkley was offered another ship but turned it down, insisting it was "too small to keep to the sea." He subsequently faded from history. Campbell, it seems, left the British Navy and threw his lot in with the Spaniards, though he later denied such claims.

Over 250 years later, it is Byron who is perhaps the most famous crewmember. He was promoted to Master and Commander, and given the command of the *Syren*. He lived a long life, during which he sailed around the world before his death in 1786. He was also married and had a number of children whom he lived to see grow up. They in turn had children of their own, one of whom grew up to be one of Britain's most famous Romantic poets: Lord Byron. The dashing young poet certainly had a spirit as adventurous as his legendary grandfather, and he would suffer trials and tribulations in war as well, dying in Greece while fighting against the Turks in the Greek War of Independence.

Lord Byron

For decades following the loss of the *Wager*, Spain controlled the area in which the ship was wrecked and was not terribly inclined to allow English explorers in to look for her. Archaeologist Diego Carabias Amor wrote that, sometime around 1743, "the Governor of Chiloe…organiz[ed] an important salvage operation to recover the guns, anchors and nautical gear of the Wager, all of which were very scarce in the region…. The objects recovered included ten iron six-pounder and four bronze three-pounder guns, an anchor, over a hundred cannon balls, over a thousand musket shot, three copper cauldrons, and various pieces of lead, iron and steel."

Having gotten all that they could use from the ship, the Spanish quickly lost interest in the wreck, and it was allowed to remain largely unmolested in the decades that followed. Men exploring the area would occasionally make reference to finding parts of the ship, but there was no concerted effort made to explore or salvage it.

In 2006, over 250 years after the ship was wrecked, the Scientific Exploration Society asked Major Chris Holt to lead a team in search of the *Wager*. The team flew out of England on November 5 and made their way to Patagonia, accomplishing in hours what it had taken Anson and his men months to do. Once there, he tried a number of sites before demanding that the team get back to basics. He confided to his journal, "We re-read the accounts (rather than the books about the accounts) and came up with the following pieces of information that we felt were important: . The ship was only 'feet from making clear water' and missing the island before she struck. 2. When the men first launched the lengthened long-boat Speedwell, they immediately turned away from the wind and across the 'inlet' to Speedwell Bay (something in the accounts we had somehow previously all missed)."

He gleaned one more piece of critical information: "3. From Mount Misery looking towards land (i.e. east), it was not possible to see if they were on an island because of greater hills in the way. All of these points lead us to believe we need to be not on the north-eastern but on the north-western shore."

Armed with this information, the team chose a new site in which to look, at the foot of what the sailors had called Mount Misery but had later been named Mount Anson. This proved to be the right place, as Holt later wrote in his report, "Andy [Torbet] is not someone who is drawn into false optimism; he is a 'professional Scotsman' and proud of it. When I met him back at the boats, he was excited about the correlation between what he had seen from the top of the mountain and the descriptions in the accounts. He finished off his debrief to me by saying: 'I think I've just been to the summit of Mount Misery, which means that the Wager is somewhere here.'"

Excited by this prediction, the entire team moved about their tasks quickly until one member cried out in pain after he had stubbed his toe on something. He called out to the others, "Just a minute fellas, I'm going to move this damned thing, otherwise I'll only do it again."

Holt described what happened next: "On his hands and knees, he cleared away the sand around the offending item and tried to move it away from his now throbbing toes. It was an unusual moment, one of those where everyone goes quiet at the same time and you cannot really remember who spoke first, but, as he continued to fan with his hand, slowly but surely the outline of a large worked piece of timber became visible…More hands joined his, and within three or four minutes we had uncovered about one and a half metres of hull planking. An unusual feeling came over me, much like when you have known the answer to a question all along, but for some reason have forgotten to tell anyone. We were literally ten metres away from my tent, in the very spot where for a week we had been washing our pots, pans, clothes and bodies, and it was entirely likely that we had just stumbled over the wreck of HMS Wager…The storm that had come close to washing away our morale had also scoured away large amounts of sand on the bottom of the stream, exposing the smallest edge of timbers that must have remained buried for decades."

There was too little time and not enough provisions to do more than excavate what they could and take some pictures. The site was visited again the following year, and more of the wreckage was found, but for the most part, the *Wager* still keeps her own counsel and lies, like the bodies of so many of her crew, on the shore and in the shallow waters off the Chilean coast.

Online Resources

Other books about British history by Charles River Editors

Other books about the HMS Wager on Amazon

Bibliography

Anon. *An Affecting Narrative of the Unfortunate Voyage and Catastrophe of His Majesty's Ship Wager*. London: J. Norwood, 1751.

John Bulkley and John Cummins. *A Voyage to the South-Seas in the Years 1740-1*. London: Jacob Robinson, 1743. Second edition, with additions, London, 1757.

John Byron. *Narrative of the Hon. John Byron; Being an Account of the Shipwreck of The Wager; and the Subsequent Adventures of Her Crew*, 1768. Second edition, 1785.

Alexander Campbell. *The sequel to Bulkeley and Cummins's voyage to the South-seas*. London: W. Owen, 1747.

Isaac Morris. *Narrative of the Dangers and Distresses which befel Isaac Morris and seven more of the crew*. London: S. Birt, 1752.

Pack, S. W. C. (1964). *The Wager Mutiny*. A. Redman.

Somerville, Henry Boyle Townshend (1934). *Commodore Anson's Voyage into the South Seas and Around the World*. W. Heinemann.

Free Books by Charles River Editors

We have brand new titles available for free most days of the week. To see which of our titles are currently free, click on this link.

Discounted Books by Charles River Editors

We have titles at a discount price of just 99 cents everyday. To see which of our titles are currently 99 cents, click on this link.

Made in the USA
Columbia, SC
20 March 2025